Of Gods and Goddess

Acknowledgements

Grateful acknowledgement is made to the following for permission to use copyright material:

The Bodley Head for "Thor's Unlucky Journey" from *Thunder of the Gods* by Dorothy Hosford. Published by The Bodley Head/ The British and Foreign Bible Society for "The Story of the Creation" from Genesis 1 and 2 vv 1–4 from *The Good News Bible*— Old Testament: copyright © American Bible Society 1976/Christ's College, Cambridge for "The Story of Perseus" from *Gods, Heroes and Men of Ancient Greece* by W. H. D. Rouse. Copyright the Master, Fellows and Scholars of Christ's College, Cambridge/Louise H. Schlove for "Ancient History" from *Lyric Laughter* by Arthur Guiterman. Used by permission of Louise H. Schlove/Harold Ober Associates Incorporated, for the poem "Pegasus" from *The Children's Bells*. Reprinted by permission of Harold Ober Associates Incorporated. Copyright © 1957 by Eleanor Farjeon/ Heinemann Educational Books for "The Light and the Souls": Chapters 1 and 2 from *Myths and Legends of the Swahili* by Jan Knappert; also for "The Revolt Against God" from *African Creation Myths*, edited by Ulli Beier/ Holt, Rinehart and Winston Inc. for "Some say the sun is a golden earring" and "The thunder is a great dragon" from *The Sun is a Golden Earring* by Natalia M. Belting. Copyright © 1962 by Natalia M. Belting. Reprinted by permission of Holt, Rinehart and Winston Inc./ Houghton Mifflin Company for "The Apples of Idun" from *Legends of the North* by Olivia Coolidge. Copyright © 1951 by Olivia Coolidge. Reprinted by permission of Houghton Mifflin Company.

Every effort has been made to obtain permission for copyright material and the publishers would be grateful for any discrepancies to be notified.

Editorial consultants
James Britton/Diana Bentley/Fran Oliver/ Pat Parsons/Betty Root/Anne Rogers.

Level 12 artists
Don Albright/Victor Ambrus/Ramon Ameijide/ Leon Baxter/Val Biro/Ben Black/Mike Cassaro/Diane and Leo Dillon/Tony Heald/ Lin Jenkins/Judy and Todd McKie/David McPhail/Jane Oka/Joan Paley/Don Pulver/ William Papas/George Salonovich/Graham Smith/Lynn Sweat/Garth Williams

Published by Ginn and Company Ltd
Prebendal House, Parson's Fee, Aylesbury, Bucks HP20 2QZ

Printed in Great Britain by Ebenezer Bayis & Son Ltd
The Trinity Press, Worcester, and London

Contents

The ancient Greeks thought that disaster would befall a mortal who displeased one of the gods. Good fortune was the destiny of those whom the gods favoured. Thus the people of ancient Greece believed in cause and effect.

What happened that caused two beautiful trees to stand alone above a marsh? You will discover how this question was answered by the people of ancient Greece.

BAUCIS AND PHILEMON

On a certain hill in the pleasant land of Greece, there stands a linden tree and an oak. A low wall circles them. Not far from this spot is a marsh. It was once good, fertile land, but now it is fit only for marsh birds and cormorants. This is a tale the ancients told of how that marsh and those two trees came to be.

Once upon a time, Zeus visited this country along with his son Hermes. Pretending to be weary travellers, they presented themselves at many a door, seeking rest and shelter. It was late and all the doors were closed. And though the gods banged and called, the sleepy families inside would not bother to leave their beds to let the travellers in.

So Zeus and Hermes wandered on until, a bit beyond the wealthy town, they came to a very humble little cottage. It was small with a thatched roof and a door so low that Zeus had to stoop to knock upon it.

"Who's there? Who's there?" called a voice from within.

"Weary travellers wanting food and a place to sleep," cried Hermes, who was very tired and hungry by this time.

Almost at once the door was flung open and an old man stood peering out at the two strangers. "Come in," he said, "you are welcome here."

Zeus and Hermes, stooping, entered the little cottage. A soft light greeted them from the fireside where an old woman was stirring the embers to make the flames spring up again.

"Here are two weary travellers wanting food and a place to sleep," her husband said to her. "Can we manage to put something before them?"

The wife came hurrying over. She spread a rough cloth on the one bare table. Then on it she placed black bread and cheese. The husband reached down a piece of bacon hanging from the roof rafters and the old wife cut it up and put it over the fire to boil. Then she brought water in a basin so that the travellers could refresh themselves before eating.

When the bacon was ready, the old man bade Zeus and Hermes to come at once to the table. He made no apologies for the very simple supper, for it was what he ate every day. He was only sharing what food he had.

The gods seated themselves and began to put the cheese and the bacon onto the wooden plates before them. They reached for the earthen pitcher to pour the goats' milk into their earthen mugs.

Then a strange thing happened. As Zeus picked up a piece of the coarse black bread, it became fine-grained and as white as snow. The wooden plate began to glow in the firelight, as if it were made of gold. Indeed, it was suddenly changed to pure gold. The goats' milk turned into red wine and the earthen mug was changed into clearest crystal.

At the sight of this, the old man,

whose name was Philemon, flung himself down on his knees, for now the travellers had revealed themselves as gods. The whole cottage shone with their glory. Baucis, the wife, also fell to her knees, and both the old people trembled with terror. With clasped hands they begged their guests to forgive the humble food which was all they had to put before them.

"I will kill the goose," declared Philemon. "I was saving it to celebrate our wedding anniversary, but you shall have it."

"Yes, yes," cried old Baucis.

They started after the goose which they kept in the cottage at night to protect it from wolves and foxes. But the goose, startled out of its sleep, flapped its wings and ran around the room, at last taking shelter on the crude bench between the two gods.

Zeus put his hand upon the goose and quieted it. "No, you shall not kill the goose. Keep it to celebrate your wedding anniversary. We are gods indeed. I am Zeus and this is my son,

Hermes." He rose from the bench. "Now come with us to the top of the hill just beyond here."

The old couple followed the gods out of the cottage and into the night. Slowly they began to climb the hill. When they neared its top, Zeus said, "Look below."

Baucis and Philemon turned. What a sight met their eyes! The moon had risen and they could see plainly. Where once the fair town had stood there was now only water with marsh grasses growing around its edge. The only building in sight was their own humble

little cottage.

While they stood, wondering and sad at the terrible fate of their neighbours, suddenly they saw their cottage change. Its thatched roof rose, then disappeared, and shining tiles shone in the moonlight. White pillars appeared where once the low door had been. Their cottage was transformed into a *temple*. A temple of the gods!

Then Zeus spoke in a gentle tone. "Kindly old man, and woman fit for such a husband, tell us what your wishes are. Ask anything you want, and it shall be granted to you."

The old couple whispered together for a moment and then Philemon spoke. "We ask to be priests and guardians of this, your temple. And since we have passed our lives together in love and peace, we desire that we may die at the same moment. Let our graves be side by side."

Their wish was granted. Baucis and Philemon lived out the rest of their lives tending the temple which had been raised where their humble dwelling had stood.

Then one day, as they stood on the steps of the temple, Baucis saw Philemon begin to sprout leaves. Philemon saw Baucis changing in the same way.

"Goodbye, my dear wife," whispered Philemon.

"Goodbye, dear husband," she whispered back.

Suddenly two beautiful trees appeared, one an oak, the other a linden.

Thus did two great gods reward the kindness of two good people.

ARACHNE

Athena, after whom the city of Athens was named, was the goddess of wisdom and such fine arts as weaving. She demanded the highest respect from earthbound mortals. According to Greek mythology, Athena gave help and gifts to those who worshipped her.

But then came Arachne! What natural phenomenon does her strange fate explain?

In very olden times, there lived in Greece a girl named Arachne. She was known throughout the land because of her great skill at weaving. No person on earth, it was said, could weave as skilfully as she. There were some who said not even Athena, goddess of wisdom and the household arts, could weave as well as Arachne. Among those who boasted arrogantly was Arachne herself.

No, this girl was not modest about her skill. She was foolishly proud of it and even made fun of the work of girls less gifted than she. But then, one had to admit it was a wondrous sight to see her fingers moving lightly and swiftly back and forth across her loom. Her designs were intricate and beautiful, and she wove the colours of her threads with the ease and smoothness of an artist working with brush and paint. So graceful was she in all her motions that often the wood nymphs left their shadowy hiding places to watch her at work.

In time Arachne's fame and her boasting reached the ears of Athena, and the goddess decided to draw the girl into a contest that would cure her of her arrogant pride. So one day when Arachne was weaving in a pleasant grove, there suddenly appeared beside her a bent old woman. She gazed for a moment at Arachne's loom, then said, "That is a pretty piece of weaving, my dear, and yet I have seen the time in my youth when I could have done as well."

At this Arachne threw up her head and said in a scornful tone, "Never did any mortal weave as I am weaving now, old woman."

"Those are rash words," said the old woman, and a strange angry light came into her grey eyes, which were exceedingly youthful for one so bent with years. "It is foolish to take too great a pride in what one can do, for surely there is always someone who can do the task even better."

"Not so," cried the angry girl. "There is no one who can weave better than I."

The old woman smiled and shook her head doubtfully. "Allowing that no mortal can weave as well as you, at least among the immortals there is one who can surpass you in the art."

Arachne left off her weaving to stare at the old woman. "And who is that, pray?" she asked.

"The goddess Athena," replied the old woman.

Arachne laughed scornfully. "Not even Athena can weave as well as I."

At these words, the wood nymphs, who had on this occasion as on so many others come to watch

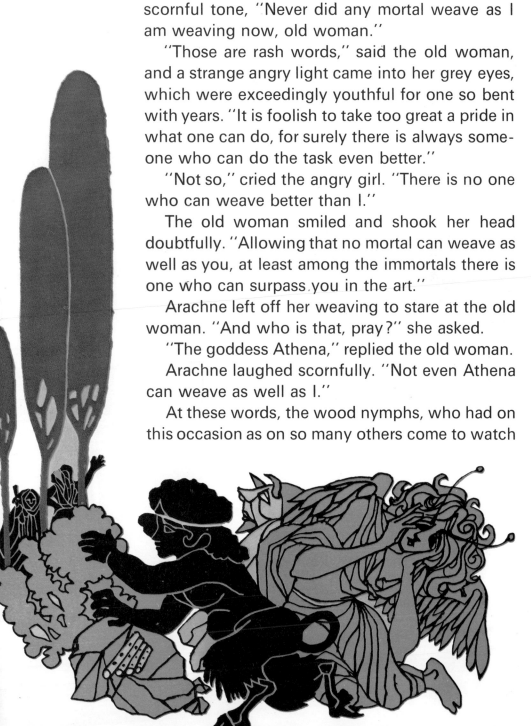

Arachne, began to whisper among themselves. They were very frightened, for it was highly dangerous for any mortal to set himself above the gods in anything. Foolish Arachne!

On hearing the boastful words, the old woman's eyes again flashed angrily. But in a moment they softened, and she said, "You are young and have spoken foolishly and in haste. Surely you did not mean what you said. I will give you a chance to take back your words."

But Arachne again flung up her head defiantly. "I did mean what I said, and I shall prove it."

"Prove it then," cried the old woman in a terrible voice. In the next instant, a cry went up from the circling crowd, and Arachne's face turned as white as a sheet. For the old woman had vanished and in her place stood the shining form of the goddess Athena.

"For a long time," she said, "I have listened to your boastings and have watched your growing vanity. Now it has led you to defy the very gods. It is time you received a lesson from which other mortals as foolish and as vain as you may profit. Let the contest begin."

Another loom was set up in the pleasant grove and Arachne and the goddess began to weave. News of the contest spread through the quiet meadow and up

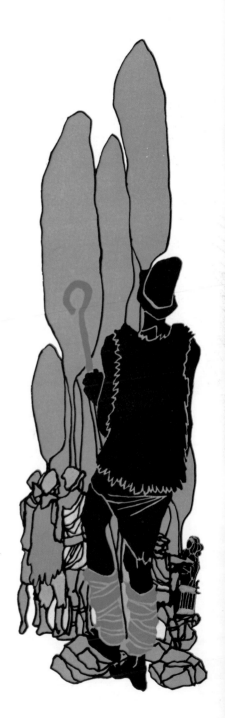

to the mountain heights. Soon a large crowd of shepherds drew near to watch the weavers. What they saw was worth coming far to see.

Athena wove upon her loom a bright tapestry which told the story of other foolish mortals who had thought themselves greater than the gods and who had been punished for their pride. Arachne pictured on her loom the stories which told of the foolish acts of the gods themselves, for it was well known among mortals that the gods did not always behave wisely.

The colours used by the two weavers were so bright that they might have been plucked from the rainbow. The weaving was so perfect that the figures on each loom seemed to be alive and breathing. The watchers marvelled that such skill could be displayed on earth or in heaven.

At last the tapestries were finished and the two contestants stood back to see what each had wrought upon her loom. At the sight of Arachne's finished work, Athena was so angered by what the girl had dared to picture there, that she struck the tapestry with her shuttle, splitting it in two. Then she struck Arachne on the forehead. Immediately there swept over the girl a deep sense of her vanity in setting herself above the very gods. So great was her shame that she went at once and hanged herself. But when Athena beheld her lifeless body, she took pity upon the foolish Arachne.

"Live," she said, "but never must you be allowed to forget the lesson you have learned today. Though you may live, you must hang throughout all eternity —you and all who come after you and are of your flesh and blood."

With that, she sprinkled Arachne with bitter juices. At once her hair and ears and nose disappeared. Her whole body shrank, her arms and legs too. Her head grew small, and she took the shape of what we now call the spider. From her body she drew the thread with which she spun her web. And often we come upon her hanging by that thread just as Athena said she must hang throughout all eternity.

PHAETHON

The ancient Greeks believed that the great sun-god, Phoebus Apollo, drove his fiery chariot across the sky from dawn to dusk. Here again a myth explained the wonders of nature which fascinated and puzzled the Greeks. It also told of Phaethon, son of Phoebus Apollo, and the awful request he made of his father. What terrifying thing happened as a result of this request? Read the myth to find the answer.

The Greeks believed that their gods dwelt on the top of a high mountain called Olympus. Among them was Phoebus Apollo, god of music and medicine as well as god of the sun. It was he who drove the fiery chariot, drawn by four winged horses, across the sky each day. Every morning, heading out from the Gates of Dawn, Phoebus drove his chariot up into the sky and straight across the heavens, until at last he reached the spot where his course descended into the western ocean and Night arrived.

The sun-god's palace was a splendid dwelling. Its golden walls dazzled the eyes. Its lofty columns were of glowing bronze, and its doors of gleaming silver.

Now, to this shining palace there came one day a youth named Phaethon. He approached the silver doors slowly, pausing frequently to clear his eyes which were dazzled by all the brilliance. Still he pressed on because he had a question to put to the sun-god. His mother, a mortal named Clymene, had told Phaethon that Phoebus Apollo was his father. But when the boy boasted to his playmates that his father was a god, they scoffed at him and said, "Prove it."

And thus Phaethon was standing in the very throne room of the great palace where the god Phoebus sat, his radiant crown upon his head. Around him stood his attendants ranged in appointed order. Here were the Days, the Months, the Years and, at regular intervals, the Hours. The Seasons were present too: Spring in a garland of flowers, Summer cradling a sheaf of wheat, Autumn with wine-stained feet and Winter wearing a hoary cap of ice.

The sun-god, who sees everything, soon noticed Phaethon standing there, his sight almost blinded by the splendour.

Phoebus looked kindly upon the boy and asked, "What has brought you here?"

And Phaethon answered boldly, "I have come to ask if you are in truth my father. My mother, Clymene, has told me so, but my friends laugh when I claim to be your son. And so I have come to ask you if it is true and, if so, to grant me

proof."

As Phaethon spoke, Phoebus removed the glittering crown from his head so that the boy might more easily gaze upon him. Then, reaching out, he took Phaethon tenderly into his arms and drew him close.

"Phaethon, Clymene, your mother, has spoken the truth. I am indeed your father and to prove it, ask anything of me and I swear by the river Styx that your wish will be granted."

Now, no god could swear by the river Styx and go back upon his oath. It was the highest vow a god could take. And Phoebus had taken this great oath to grant Phaethon anything he wished, whatever it might be.

Phaethon had his answer ready. He knew of the sun-god's journey each day

across the sky. He well knew how all peoples of the earth counted upon seeing the fiery chariot and its galloping horses as they cleared the Gates of Dawn, sending light and warmth to the earth below.

So now Phaethon cried, "I choose to take your place, Father. For this one day let me drive your winged chariot across the sky. Just this one day."

Too late, Phoebus realized his own folly. Fear and sorrow shadowed the god's shining face. Why had he made a reckless promise and bound himself to grant whatever foolish wish might enter a boy's rash young head?

At last he said, "Dear lad, this is the only wish I would have refused you. If I could only take back my promise! For you have to do what no one can achieve but me. Not even Zeus, hurler of thunderbolts, can drive my chariot. And no one is as powerful as he. Let me tell you of the danger you face. The road is steep, so steep that the horses can hardly climb it though they are fresh in the morning. It runs high across the middle heavens, so high that even I am frightened when I look down and see the earth and sea beneath me. At last it descends as sharply as it rose in the beginning. I must hold the horses on a tight rein. Added to all this, the sky is always spinning and the

stars whirl with it. I can drive successfully against all this. What would you do? Suppose I should lend you the chariot. Could you keep the course while the world was whirling under you?

"Besides all this, the road runs through the midst of frightening monsters, the Bull, the Lion, the Scorpion and the Crab.

"Renounce your wish while you can. Do you want proof that you are my son? I give you that proof in my fears for you. Look at my face. I would you could see into my heart and could there see a father's fears.

"Look around the world. Choose whatever you will of what earth and sea contain. It shall be yours. I swear it. Only do not ask what you have asked."

He ended. But the youth persisted with his demand.

Phaethon pleaded with his father, reminding him that he had sworn the most sacred oath that even a god could take. Phoebus Apollo was forced to consent to the lad's mad wish. Sorrowfully he took Phaethon's hand and led him to where the shining chariot waited.

While Phaethon stood admiring the great beauty of its craftsmanship, Dawn woke in the east and flung wide her doors. The stars faded. The sun-god watched as the moon vanished from the sky. Then he ordered the Hours to harness

up the horses. They obeyed, leading the animals from their stalls. Then the harness was put in place and the sun-god annointed his son's face so that he could endure the chariot's heat. Next Apollo placed the dazzling crown upon young Phaethon's head.

"My son," he said, "listen to a few last words of warning and heed them. Use the whip seldom and hold the reins tightly. These horses go fast enough on their own. Your work will be to hold them in. You will see the marks of the wheels and they shall guide you. Do not go too high or too low. The middle course is the safest and the best. Now I leave you to your own luck. May it plan better for you than you have done for yourself."

While he was talking, Phaethon leaped into the chariot. He grasped the reins with delight, pouring out thanks to his reluctant father.

The moment for starting had come. The doors were flung open and the horses rushed upon the sky, swinging the chariot aloft behind them. Their galloping hoofs parted the morning mist and outran the morning breezes which had sprung up in the east.

Suddenly the horses became aware that all was not as it usually was. The load in the chariot was lighter. The feel of the reins was different too. The horses soon realized that another driver was trying to control them. They began to run where they wished, up and down, here and there, leaving the travelled road. Phaethon, frightened, did not know how to guide them. Even had he known, he did not have the power to force his will upon them.

When the unlucky boy looked down upon the earth now spreading beneath him, he grew pale. His knees shook with terror and his eyes grew dim. He wished he had never touched his father's horses. What should he do? Much of the road lay behind him, but more remained before. His courage gone, Phaethon let the reins fall from his hands. The horses, feeling the reins loose upon their backs, dashed headlong into unknown regions of the sky. Now they were high in the heavens, now down to earth. The clouds smoked and the mountaintops caught on fire. The very rivers began to dry up from

the fierce heat. The sea shrank up. Phaethon, surrounded by the fire and smoke, with the floor of the chariot burning his feet, longed to be rid of this terror.

At last Earth herself sent up a plea to Zeus. "Save us, Father," she cried. "Save what remains to us."

Zeus heard her plea, and seizing his thunderbolt hurled it at the young driver. Phaethon, his hair on fire, fell headlong like a shooting star which marks the heavens with its brightness as it falls.

A great river received his burning body and put out its fire. And the river nymphs buried him, marking his grave with a stone which bore these words:

Phaethon rests beneath this stone.
He tried to drive his father's chariot,
And though he failed,
Yet brave was his try.

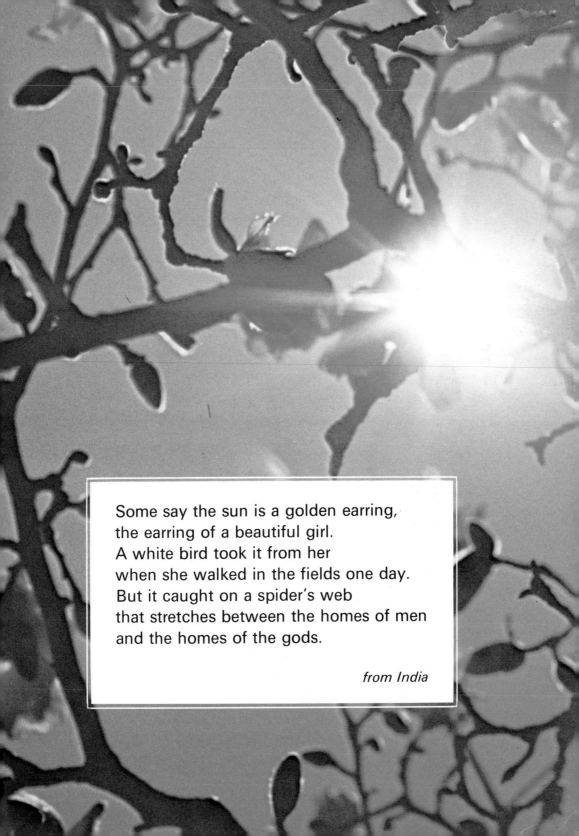

Some say the sun is a golden earring,
the earring of a beautiful girl.
A white bird took it from her
when she walked in the fields one day.
But it caught on a spider's web
that stretches between the homes of men
and the homes of the gods.

from India

THE STORY OF PERSEUS

In Greek mythology one of the great heroes was Perseus, son of Zeus, the ruler of all the gods, and Danae, a mortal woman. The name Zeus was sometimes spelt Seus. In the Latin language the prefix per means through. So Perseus was a son through Zeus. The story which follows tells about the great and daring deeds of this mortal son as he searched for the terrible Medusa, whose hair was curling ringlets of snakes.

Danae and the Shower of Gold

In the days of the gods, there lived in Greece a king named Acrisios. He was rich and powerful, but still a most unhappy man. An oracle had foretold that King Acrisios would one day be killed by his own grandson.

At the time of this oracle, Acrisios did not have a grandson. But he did have a beautiful daughter named Danae. She was so lovely that many men had already sought her hand in marriage. The possibility that Acrisios would someday have a grandson was all too real, and so the frightened king took steps to prevent this.

He built a strong tower of brass and had poor Danae shut up inside it along with her waiting-women, and he allowed no one else to go in.

This was a cruel fate, and Danae was very unhappy. But what could she do? No one dared to come in, and the attendants and guards were much too afraid of the king to allow anyone to visit her.

But Zeus, ruler of the gods, who sees all things, saw Danae in her tower. And as she was beautiful, Zeus fell in love with her, resolving to make her his wife. It was easy enough for him, but he did not march up to the door and demand admittance. He made another plan, quite a new one.

So it happened that one day as Danae sat melancholy in her chamber at the top of the tower, she saw the air become thick with a kind of mist. Soon the mist grew into soft flakes of gold, like golden snow, and fell all over the room. The flakes gathered up into a solid shape. And she saw standing before her what she thought was a noble young man, and his body was covered with bright clothing that shone like gold.

"Who are you?" said Danae, astonished.

"Do not fear me," said he, "for I have heard of your sad fate, and I have come to comfort you if you will be my wife."

Danae was delighted to have so noble a husband when she expected none at all, not even an ugly one. So after that, Zeus would often come and visit her in a shower of golden snowflakes, unknown to all, and after his visit he would melt into golden snowflakes again and pass away on the wind.

Acrisios knew nothing of all this. So imagine his amazement one day when a messenger came panting before him, and said:

"Sir, your daughter has borne a son!"

"What!" cried Acrisios. "Did I not forbid you to let anyone go in?"

"Sir," he answered, "we have let no one go in. We know nothing about it! Do not blame us, we have done our duty, I swear it."

Then Acrisios was angry and frightened at once. Whatever the cause, there was his grandson, and the oracle said he was to kill Acrisios one day. Acrisios did not like to murder his daughter and the baby outright. But he quieted his conscience by saying that they should have a chance. So he put them into a large chest with holes to let in the air, and fastened the lid. And then he set them adrift on the sea.

The winds blew and the waves rose, and the foam drenched the mother and her son as they lay in the chest. The tears ran down her cheeks, and she threw her arms about the boy and said, "Ah, my baby, what sorrow is yours! And yet you weep not. You sleep quietly like a suckling babe in this dark chest. You care

not for the salt foam on your hair nor for the whistling wind as you lie in your purple wrappings with your soft cheek against mine. If you knew your danger, you would open your little ear to my words. Sleep on, my babe, and may the sea sleep, and may Zeus your father send us help!"

Perseus and the Gorgon Medusa

Zeus heard the mother's prayer. The chest was washed up on the shore of a little island named Seriphos. An islander came by and saw the chest, which was richly carved, and he thought it a great find. But when he prised open the lid, he was surprised to see Danae and the baby inside! He was a kind man, and took them in, and they lived in his house while the boy grew up.

The boy's name was Perseus; and he grew up to be strong and brave and handsome, and he won prizes in the athletic games of the island. So he was noticed by the king, Polydectes. Before long the king caught sight of Perseus's mother, Danae, and determined to make her his wife.

But Danae would not hear of it. She, the wife of the immortal Zeus, to give herself to the petty chief of a small island! The king persecuted her, but he was afraid of Perseus; and he soon saw that he must rid himself of Perseus.

Accordingly, he pretended to flatter him on his success in the games. "You are a fine boy," Polydectes said. "You can beat everyone on this island at running, boxing and wrestling. In fact, you are wasted in a small place like this. You ought to try some great task and make a name in the world, like the real heroes." You see, he did not know that Perseus was a real hero, being a son of Zeus. Danae kept that secret to herself.

"What do you mean, sir?" asked Perseus. "Just tell me something worth trying for."

"I will," said the king. "Go and bring me Medusa's head."

Perseus asked, "Who is Medusa?"

The king said, "There are three awful sisters, the three Gorgons. Two of them are ugly things, but the Gorgon Medusa is the most beautiful creature in the world. I want her head, never mind why."

"Where can they be found?" asked Perseus.

The king said, "Far away in the west, in the land of darkness. You must find your own way, for I do not know any more about it."

This fired Perseus with ambition, and he determined to fetch Medusa's head.

The gods knew all this, of course, and as Perseus was thinking what to do, Athena suddenly appeared to him.

"Perseus, do you know me?" she asked.

"Indeed I do!" said Perseus. "You are the great goddess Athena."

"Well," said Athena, "we gods are going to help you. First of all, look at this," and she showed him the image of a head. The face was very beautiful, but cruel and cold and unhappy. Instead of hair, it had curling ringlets of snakes all round. "That is the Gorgon Medusa," Athena said. "But if you look at the real face, you will be turned into stone."

"Then how can I get the head?" asked Perseus.

"Take this shield," and she gave him a shield, smooth and shining like a mirror, "and when you come to Medusa, keep your back to her and look at her image in the shield, so as to strike back over your shoulder. Then cut off her head and put it in this bag," and she gave him a large leather bag. "Be careful to leave her sisters alone, for they are immortal. Medusa alone is mortal, and she can be killed."

"But how shall I find the way?" he asked.

"Wait a moment," said Athena, and then all of a sudden, there stood Hermes and Hades, who appeared out of nothing, as the gods can do. But Hermes said, "See here, I will lend you my winged shoes. Put them on your feet and you will fly through the air like a bird. And here is a sharp sickle to cut off Medusa's head." Then Hades said, "And I will lend you my cap of darkness. When you wear it, you will be invisible and no one will see you."

"And now," said Athena, "you must fly away to the west until you come to the Three Old Hags, who alone know the way to the Gorgons. They have only one eye between them, and one tooth, which they lend between them as they want them. They live in the west beyond the sun and moon, and you will have to persuade them to tell you the way."

This did not sound hopeful, but there was no more to be done, as the three gods had disappeared.

So Perseus slung the shield and the sickle over his shoulders and hung the bag over his back. He put on the cap of darkness and fastened the winged shoes to his feet. Then he rose into the air. For a few moments he ran along in the air trying out the shoes, and his feet felt light and tireless and he smiled with joy to be running in the air. Then he started out to find the

Three Old Hags.

On and on he flew, over land and sea, over mountain and forest, beyond the sun and the moon into the dark regions of the west. No doubt the winged shoes guided him, for he came straight to the place where the Three Old Hags had their dwelling.

One said to her sister, "I hear a noise in the air. What is it?"

The second answered, "Give me the tooth, and let me bite it." So the tooth was passed to her, but she could see nothing as the eye was in the socket of the third.

The first asked, "Sister, what can you see?"

And she answered, "I can see nothing at all, but I hear a shivering in the air." For the cap of darkness made Perseus invisible.

"Pass me the eye!" said the first sister. "You are as blind as a bat!" She put the eye into her own socket but saw nothing. Then the second sister said, "Pass it here, will you?"

But as the first sister took out the eye and held it towards the other, Perseus neatly swooped in between them and caught it. "Now then," said the first sister, "can you see anything?" for she thought that her sister had taken the eye.

They quarrelled back and forth until at last the second sister said, "Here, take the tooth and give her a nip."

But as she held out the tooth, Perseus swooped down quickly and caught it. Then there was a frightful quarrel as each Old Hag thought that the others were playing a trick on her. In the midst of it, Perseus called out:

"Fear nothing, mighty beings, the eye and the tooth are safe. I hold them in my hand."

There was a sudden silence. Then they all cried out at once, "Who is that?"

He replied, "I am Perseus, and I come to ask you the way to the place where the Gorgons are."

"We will not tell you," they all cried out.

"Then I will not give you back the eye and the tooth. Goodbye," and he made as if to go.

"Wait, wait, wait!" they cried. They did their best to persuade Perseus to give back the eye and the tooth, but he was firm, and in the end they had to tell him the way to go. Then he flew off saying, "When I come back, you shall have your eye and your tooth safe and sound."

Thus the Three Old Hags could not defend their sisters, the Gorgons, and Perseus came to the place where they were.

He found the Gorgons asleep. Two of them had golden wings and bronze claws and enormous teeth. They would have made short work of Perseus if they had caught him, but he was careful to be quiet. Approaching Medusa backwards, he looked at her image in the bright shield and struck a blow behind him and killed her. Then he cut off the head and put it into his bag. The two sisters awoke and tried to catch Perseus in their claws. But he was too quick for them. He flew back to the Three Old Hags and gave them the eye in turn and let them have a look at him when he took off his cap. He gave back the tooth, but took care to give it back just as he was about to fly away. And he gave it to the one who had not got the eye at that moment.

Perseus and Andromeda

The journey back was more roundabout. No doubt Perseus thought he would never have a better chance of seeing the world. He seems to have flown over Africa and Asia, and he even visited the people who lived behind the North Wind. These were a very happy people, who had a kind of earthly paradise, almost as good as the Islands of the Blest where all the great heroes went and lived forever at peace.

As he passed over Africa, he saw a huge figure with its head in the clouds, and when he looked closer, he saw that it was old Atlas the Titan, holding up the heavens upon his shoulder.

Old Atlas hailed him and said, "Stranger, you must be the hero Perseus who, according to the oracle, will set me free. Show me the Gorgon's head!" He was weary of holding up the heavens. Perseus took the head out of his bag and held it out towards Atlas, but he was careful to turn his own head away. Then he put it back in the bag. And when he looked at Atlas, he saw that his body had changed into a great rock. His hair and beard were changed into forests. So Atlas rested at last from his long labour. If you look on the map, there you will see the Atlas Mountains still, and they hold up the heavens quite as well as the old Titan did.

As Perseus came nearer to home on a bright, sunny day, he looked down. There on the coast of Palestine, near the port of Joppa, he saw a long procession of people moving towards the sea. They were leading a beautiful maiden and they bound her fast with chains to a rock and went away weeping and wailing.

The maiden's name was Andromeda and she was the daughter of the king of that place. Her mother was a vain and foolish woman and she had boasted that her daughter was more beautiful than all the nymphs of the sea. Accordingly, the god of the sea, Poseidon, the father of these nymphs, was very angry. He flooded the coast and sent a sea monster to devour anyone he could catch. At last, after many prayers, he consented to spare the people if the king would give his daughter to the sea monster to devour. That was why they left her chained to a rock and went away.

Perseus did not know this. He only saw the maiden chained to a rock and an ugly monster swimming in from the sea. The maiden stared at the monster, her eyes full of horror. The monster lashed the sea with his tail, and his green sides shone in the sunlight with scales of hard horn. His mouth opened to display a red throat and sharp rows of teeth. Neither he nor Andromeda looked up to see a new kind of bird swoop down from the sky. Down came Perseus, like an eagle, holding the sickle of Hermes which had cut off the Gorgon's head. He attacked the monster from behind and gave him a deep cut on the neck. Then there was a terrible fight. But the monster could not reach Perseus who flew in and out like an eagle, cutting under the monster's scales, until at last he cut its throat and the body fell back lifeless upon the sea.

You may imagine how glad Andromeda was and how Perseus loosed her chains and led her back to her father. And how glad her father was and how willingly he consented when Perseus asked him if Andromeda

might be his wife. Had he not well earned the prize?

There was only one difficulty. The king had promised her to someone else. This was a man named Phineus, who came up in a rage and said, "Where is my bride?"

Perseus asked, "Where were you when the sea monster was going to devour your bride?"

Phineus replied, "I could not help her. Why should I be swallowed too?"

Perseus said, "If you did not care enough for your bride to strike a blow for her life, you have no claim."

"We will see about that," Phineus said. "Here, you men!" and he called to his bodyguards, who stood under arms, with threatening looks. But Perseus did not wait for more. He took out the Gorgon's head and showed it to them. There they stood, turned into stone.

There was a grand wedding and much rejoicing. But Perseus had to leave his bride for the time being because he had to go back to Seriphos and hand over the Gorgon's head to Polydectes.

When he came to Seriphos, he took off his winged shoes and walked to the town. But he could not find his mother. The fact was, King Polydectes had persecuted her and told her she must be his wife whether she liked it or not. He knew only that Perseus had gone, but he did not know how and he felt sure that he would never come back. Then Perseus found his mother in the temple where she had fled for refuge. With her was the kind man who had brought him up.

When Danae saw Perseus, she cried, "Oh, my son! You have come back, and I thought you were dead!"

"What are you doing here?" he asked.

She said, "The king was so violent and threatening

that I have fled to this temple for refuge. But I am afraid even here, for he says he will come and fetch me. And there he is!"

Indeed there he was, with his bodyguard of soldiers, come to drag Danae from the temple.

"Come out!" he cried. "My patience is at an end— But who is this? Never Perseus, returned from his journey? Welcome, dear boy!" for he began to be afraid now.

Then Perseus said, "Do not call me dear boy when you want to lay violent hands on my mother."

"Nonsense," he answered, "but tell me about your journey. Did you get the Gorgon's head?"

"Oh yes," said Perseus, "would you like to see it?"

"Indeed I should," said the king.

Then Perseus whispered to his mother, "Turn your head away," and as she turned away, he drew out the Gorgon's head and turned it towards Polydectes.

As Polydectes looked at it, a shiver ran through him, and in a moment he was a statue of stone with the smile still on his false lips. His men also turned into stone, as many as looked upon the Gorgon's head.

Perseus put the head back and led his mother to her home. The kind man who had helped them became king, and all was well.

The three immortals appeared once more to Perseus. Athena said, "I see you have got the head of Medusa, and come back safely. I am very glad to see it, and now you must return to us what we lent you."

Perseus thanked them all for their help. Then he gave the bag and the shield to Athena, and the cap to Hades, and to Hermes the sickle and winged shoes. But the head of Medusa he gave to Athena, and

Athena fixed it upon her shield. Ever after she bore the shield with the Gorgon's head. And if she showed it to her enemies, they were turned into stone.

Perseus sent for his bride and they lived a happy life. But there is one more thing that you need to know about him.

There used to be games on the island of Seriphos and once Acrisios came to attend them. Perseus had to throw a quoit at the games. It went a little to one side where Acrisios was craning his head forward to look on. The quoit caught his head and killed him. So the oracle was fulfilled which had made Acrisios so cruel to Danae.

W. H. D. Rouse

Ancient History

I hope the old Romans
Had painful abdomens.

I hope that the Greeks
Had toothache for weeks.

I hope the Egyptians
Had chronic conniptions.

I hope that the Arabs
Were bitten by scarabs.

I hope that the Vandals
Had thorns in their sandals.

I hope that the Persians
Had gout in all versions.

I hope that the Medes
Were kicked by their steeds.

They started the fuss
And left it to us!

Arthur Guiterman

Pegasus

From the blood of Medusa
Pegasus sprang.
His hoof of heaven
Like melody rang.
His whinny was sweeter
Than Orpheus' lyre,
The wing on his shoulder
Was brighter than fire.

His tail was a fountain,
His nostrils were caves,
His mane and his forelock
Were musical waves,
He neighed like a trumpet,
He cooed like a dove,
He was stronger than terror
And swifter than love.

He could not be captured,
He could not be bought,
His rhythm was running,
His standing was thought.
With one eye on sorrow
And one eye on mirth
He galloped in heaven
And gambolled on earth.

And only the poet
With wings to his brain
Can mount him and ride him
Without any rein,
The stallion of heaven
The steed of the skies,
The horse of the singer
Who sings as he flies.

Eleanor Farjeon

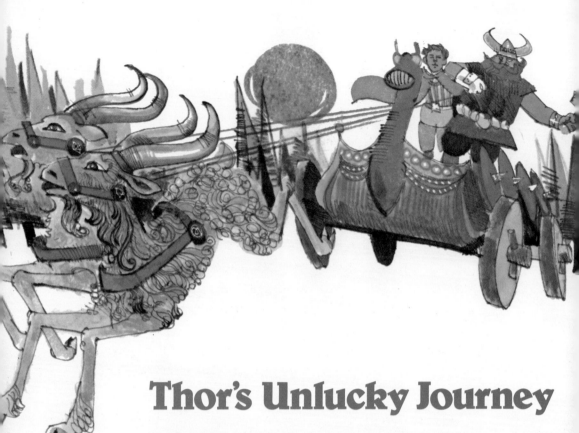

Thor's Unlucky Journey

In the Norse myths the god Odin was the ruler of all, much like Zeus in Greek mythology. Odin's son, Thor, was one of the mightiest of the gods and goddesses. The rumbling of Thor's goat-drawn chariot was said to cause thunder. What other phenomena are explained in this myth about Thor's journey to the home of the giants?

Thor, the god of thunder, was indeed one of the mightiest of the gods. His battles against the giants were many. They knew to their sorrow how great he was. Yet it cannot be said that Thor was the victor in all his encounters with the giants. There was one adventure in which he was not so lucky.

One day Thor set off in his chariot, driving his

goats. Loki went with him. Towards the end of the day they came to the house of a farmer and decided to stay there for the night. Thor's goats could always provide a meal for him. Thor slaughtered his goats and skinned them and had them cooked for supper. He invited the farmer and his wife and their son and daughter to share the meal. The name of the son was Thjalfi and the daughter was named Roskva. Thor told the farmer and his family to throw all the bones down onto the skins of the goats, when they had finished their meal. The hides were spread out on the ground a little way from the fire. They all did as they were told, except Thjalfi, who was somewhat greedy. He broke one of the bones to get at the sweet-tasting marrow.

In the morning Thor rose. He went over to the goat-skins spread on the ground. When he raised his hammer high over the bones, the goats sprang to life again. They were just as before except that one of them limped on a hind leg. When Thor saw this he knew that some-one had disobeyed him and had broken a thigh bone. His brows grew dark with anger and he gripped the handle of his hammer so fiercely that his knuckles grew white. The farmer and his family were terrified when they saw Thor's wrath.

"Have mercy, O Thor," they cried, "we will pay you for the harm we have done. We will give you our house and our cattle and our land. We will give all we own. Have mercy on us, O Mighty One."

When Thor saw how frightened they were, he forgot his anger. As payment he agreed to take the son and daughter of the farmer into his service. Thjalfi and Roskva have been with Thor ever since.

They started off again on their journey, leaving the goats behind. They walked until they came to the sea. They waded through the sea to the shore on the other side. In a little while they reached a dark forest and all day they travelled through it. Thjalfi, who was swift-footed beyond all other men, carried Thor's rucksack which contained the provisions for the journey. This was not a country in which much could be found along the way.

As it grew dark they looked about for a place to spend the night. They found a house with a wide door that stood open the whole length of the house. The house was dark and quiet and they decided to take shelter for the night. They went in and settled themselves down to sleep.

At about midnight they heard a great noise. The earth trembled as from an earthquake. They looked about for some place to hide themselves and discovered a smaller doorway leading into a side room. Loki and Thjalfi and Roskva hid themselves in the farthest corner of this room, but Thor sat in the doorway, with his hammer in his hand, ready to meet the danger.

When the light of morning came they all went outside. Roskva began to prepare breakfast. Thor said that he would walk about and have a look at things. A little way off he came upon .a huge giant stretched out asleep on the ground. He was snoring mightily and the earth shook beneath him. Then Thor knew what the rumbling and the roaring in the night had been. Thor buckled on his belt of strength, but just at that moment the giant woke and sat up. It is said that Thor, for once in his life, had no desire to strike a blow.

Instead he asked the giant what his name was. "I am called Skrymir," said the giant, "but I have no need to ask your name. I know well that you are Asa-Thor. But what have you done with my glove?"

As he spoke he stooped and picked up a great glove lying at some distance on the ground. This was what Thor and the others had mistaken in the dark for a house. The smaller doorway into the side room was the opening into the thumb.

"Shall we travel together?" said the giant.

Thor agreed. First they had breakfast, each party eating from its own provisions.

Then Skrymir suggested that they put all the food into one sack. Thor agreed. So Skrymir put Thor's rucksack into his sack. He tied the mouth of the sack and flung it over his shoulder.

They started on their journey. Skrymir strode ahead of them with such long strides that it was not easy to keep up with him. They travelled all day. When night came Skrymir found them a place to rest under a wide-spreading oak tree. He flung the sack from his shoulder to the ground.

"Now I am going to sleep," said Skrymir. "You can take your supper from the sack if you like." He lay down a little way off and at once was fast asleep.

The others were hungry. Thor began to untie the sack so that they might have some food. But though he pulled and turned and twisted the rope, the knot would not loosen at all. The more Thor struggled, the angrier he grew. Suddenly he seized his hammer with both hands. He went over to where Skrymir lay and dealt him a blow on the head.

Skrymir woke up and said, "What was that? Did a leaf fall on me? Have you had your supper, Thor?"

Thor said that they had and were getting ready to sleep. Then they went under another oak and prepared to rest, but they did not feel very safe.

At about midnight Thor heard Skrymir snoring so that the woods shook with the sound. He went over to where the giant lay and flourishing his hammer above his head, he brought it down with such force that the giant's skull was dented.

Skrymir woke up. "Now what is that?" he said. "Has an acorn fallen on me? How are things with you, Thor?"

Thor said that it was only midnight and there was still time for sleeping.

"I just happened to waken," said Thor. Then he went speedily back to his place.

Skrymir stretched out again. Thor lay quiet, but he was not asleep. He thought that if he could give Skrymir just one more blow, the giant would not see day again. Just before dawn Thor heard Skrymir snoring. Running to where he lay, Thor struck him such a mighty blow on the temple that the hammer sank into the skull up to its handle.

But Skrymir sat up and stroked his cheek. "Did a twig fall on my face? Are you awake, Thor? It is almost day, and time we were on our way."

They prepared to start their journey. Then Skrymir said, "You haven't got far to go now to reach the home of the giants. But let me give you a word of advice: don't brag too much of your prowess there, for Utgard-Loki and his men have little patience with the boasting of such small fellows as you. Perhaps it would be wiser if you did not go at all. Yet if you are determined to carry on, take the way to the east. My road lies north, to those mountains you see beyond you."

Skrymir flung the sack of food over his shoulder and was gone without another word. It has never been said that the others were sorry to see him go.

Thor and his companions travelled all morning. At about noon they caught sight of a great castle standing in the middle of a plain. The top of it was so high that they had to bend their heads back before they could see it. The gate to the castle was locked. Thor went up to it and tried to open it, but could not move it, so they crept in between the bars. They saw before them a huge hall and went towards it. The door was open and they went inside.

There they saw many men sitting about on benches and none of them could be called small men. Utgard-Loki, king of the giants, was among them. They went before him and saluted him. He took his time to look them over, laughing at them scornfully through his teeth.

"There is no need to ask news of a long journey," said Utgard-Loki. "Is this stripling Asa-Thor? Or am I wrong? Tell us in what you are skilled, you and your fellows. For no one is allowed to remain among us who cannot do something better than other men."

Loki, who was standing behind the others, spoke up. "There is one thing I am ready to wager at once, and that is that I can eat faster than anyone here."

"We shall soon find out," answered Utgard-Loki.

Then he shouted for a man named Logi to come to the centre of the hall to try his skill with Loki. A great trough of food was brought and placed upon the floor. Loki and Logi sat down at each end of it and began to eat with all their might. They met in the middle of the trough. Loki had eaten all the meat from the bones, but Logi had consumed the meat and the bones and the trough as well. So Loki was easily beaten at this game.

"What can that young man do?" asked Utgard-Loki, pointing to Thjalfi.

"I am willing to try a race with someone," answered Thjalfi.

"You will need to be swift of foot," said Utgard-Loki.

They all went outside. The level plain was a good place for running a race. Utgard-Loki called a small fellow named Hugi. He told him to run against Thjalfi.

They started. Hugi was so far ahead that he met Thjalfi as he turned back at the end of the course.

"You will have to stretch your legs more than that, Thjalfi, if you are to win," said Utgard-Loki. "Yet it is true that no man has come here who could run so well."

When they ran the second trial Hugi was so far ahead

that when he turned back at the end of the course, Thjalfi still had the length of a bow shot to run.

"Well run," said Utgard-Loki, "but I don't think that Thjalfi will win if you should run a third time."

Thjalfi ran the third time with all his might, and he was the swiftest of men. Yet Hugi had come to the end of the course and turned back before Thjalfi had reached the middle of it.

All agreed that Hugi had won the race.

Then they went inside the hall and Utgard-Loki asked Thor in what way he would try his skill. "We have heard great things of your prowess, Thor," said he.

"I will drink with anyone who cares to drink," said Thor.

"Very good," said Utgard-Loki. He called his servant boy to bring the great horn from which the henchmen sometimes drank.

"It is considered a good drink if you can empty this horn at one draught," said Utgard-Loki. "Some among us must drink twice, but there is no man here who cannot drain it in three draughts."

Thor took the horn. He didn't think it too large, though it seemed somewhat long. Thor was thirsty. He put the horn to his lips and took a long, deep draught. He thought to himself that he would not have to take more than one drink. But when he had to stop for breath and put the horn down he saw, to his surprise, that there was but little less in it than there had been before.

"Well," said Utgard-Loki, "that was a pretty good drink. But if anyone had told me that Asa-Thor could not drink more than this I would not have believed it. No doubt you will drain it this time."

Thor said nothing. He put his mouth to the horn again and drank for as long as he could hold his breath. When he paused it seemed to him that it had gone down even less than before. Yet at least one could now tilt the horn a little without spilling it.

"Well," said Utgard-Loki, "can you finish that in one more draught? It seems to me that you have perhaps left overmuch for the last drink. It cannot be said that you are as great here among us as you are among the gods, unless you are more skilled in other games than in this."

Thor grew angry. He put the horn to his mouth and drank with all his might. He struggled with it and drank for as long as he could, but when he had to put the horn down again, it was still almost full. Yet it could be said that a little space had been made in it. But Thor would drink no more.

"It can plainly be seen that you are not so great as we thought you were," said Utgard-Loki. "Will you try your skill at other games, since you won no praise in this one?"

"I will risk it," said Thor. "Yet I know that at home among the gods my drink would not have seemed so little."

"We have a game among us that does not amount to much," said Utgard-Loki. "Our young boys like to play it. It is to lift my cat from the floor. Indeed I would not have dared to mention it had I not seen that Asa-Thor is by no means as great as we thought he was."

There leapt forth upon the hall floor a large grey cat. Thor put one hand down under the middle of its body and stretched upwards. But the more he stretched the more the cat arched its back. Though he stretched as

high as he could the cat only lifted one foot off the floor. And Thor had to give up that game.

"The game went just as I thought it would," said Utgard-Loki. "The cat is very great, and Thor is low and little beside the huge men who are here with us."

"Call me little if you will," cried Thor, "but let anyone here come and wrestle with me. For now I am angry."

"I see no man here who would not hold it a disgrace to wrestle with you," said Utgard-Loki looking about the benches. "Let my old nurse, Elli, be called. Thor can wrestle with her if he wishes. She has thrown men who have seemed to me no less strong than Thor."

There appeared an old woman, bent with age. Thor grappled with her, but the more he struggled the firmer she stood. He could in no way throw her. She began to try some tricks of her own and Thor tottered. Then Thor went down upon one knee.

Utgard-Loki came up and bade them cease wrestling. "There is no need now," said he, "for Thor to challenge any of my men."

It was now getting on for evening. Utgard-Loki showed Thor and his companions to a seat at one of the benches. They remained throughout the night and were treated with great hospitality.

When morning came, Thor and the others rose and made ready to leave. Utgard-Loki himself came into the hall. He ordered a table set for them with every kind of food and drink. When they had eaten, he went to see them on their way. As they were about to part, Utgard-Loki said:

"What do you think, Thor, of this journey? Have you met any man mightier than yourself?"

"What I have done here will gain me small praise," answered Thor. "What troubles me most is that you will think me a man of little might."

"Now that you are out of the castle, I will tell you something," said Utgard-Loki. "If I live and prevail, Thor, you will never come into it again. This I know, by my troth, you should never have come into it at all had I known what strength you had! You nearly had us all in great peril."

Utgard-Loki went on speaking. "I have tricked you, Thor. It was I whom you met in the wood. I tied the sack of food with troll-iron, so that you could not undo it. When you went to smite me with the hammer I brought a mountain between us, though you could not see it. Otherwise the first blow would have slain me.

Do you see that mountain with the three valleys, one deeper than the others? Those are the marks of your blows.

"It was the same with the games you played against my henchmen," continued Utgard-Loki. "There you were tricked, too. Loki was hungry and he ate ravenously, but he who was called Logi was Fire and he devoured the trough as well as the meat. Thjalfi ran the race with Hugi, who is Thought—and how could Thjalfi outrun Thought?"

"And how did you trick *me*, Utgard-Loki?" said Thor.

"When you drank from the horn, Thor, it seemed to you to go down slowly. But that was a wonder I could hardly believe even when I saw. For the other end of the horn was in the sea itself, though you knew it not. When you look at the sea you will notice how the water has drawn back. From hence we shall call that the ebb tide.

"And my grey cat was not as it appeared to be. It was the Midgard Serpent itself which is twined about the whole earth. It was the same with the wrestling match. It was a marvel that you withstood so long and bent only one knee. You struggled with Old Age and all men must give in to Old Age at last.

"And now," said Utgard-Loki, "it is best that we part. It will be better for us both if you do not come here again. I will defend my castle with every trick I know, so that you shall have no power over me."

When Thor knew that he had been tricked, he seized his hammer and would have hurled it at Utgard-Loki, but the giant had disappeared. Thor turned towards the castle, intending to crush it with a blow from the hammer, but it was gone also. There was nothing before them but the green and level plain.

So Thor turned back, with the others, and made his way to Thrudvang, his own realm. Already his thoughts were busy as to how he might be revenged.

"One day," said Thor to himself, "I will seek out the Midgard Serpent. We shall see if I be 'low and little'."

Dorothy Hosford

The Apples of Idun

In Norse mythology the gods and goddesses depended upon the magic apples of Idun, the goddess of youth, to keep them from growing old. In this myth Loki uses trickery to cause the mysterious disappearance of Idun.

Allfather Odin was travelling with Loki and Honer in desolate wastes where they could find nothing to eat. "Let us go down into this valley ahead," said Loki. "The pasture looks green by the river, and we may find deer."

"I see oxen in the shade of those oaks," replied Odin. "By all means let us go down."

The gods turned their steps towards the valley, but the way was long, and the midsummer sun was at its height. Bees buzzed in the heath flowers, rabbits kicked up their heels as they fled to a safer patch of grass. Skylarks overhead filled the air with loud music. "They all feed while we stay hungry," grumbled Loki. "In Asgard we live like true gods. Here I am empty and hot, and my feet are sore. What is the use of such journeys?"

Odin smiled. "We should learn to know the earth because it is ours," he replied. "Sometimes we ride the clouds or fly on wings like the birds, but often we must travel as men do, step by step over stone after stone. We shall always remember these hills, their sandy soil, their sparse yellow flowers, their little dried pines and the green valley below."

"We shall indeed," muttered Loki. "It is a memory I could well have been spared."

Dusty and hot, the travellers entered the valley as the long summer evening was drawing on. They paused to drink at the river, but they did not linger, for they were faint with hunger, and the grass was now softer under their feet. Beneath three spreading oaks they killed an ox and busied themselves preparing their meal. A pile of dry branches was collected, the ox was cut up, water fetched and thrown into the pot. At last the three gods could sit down, their feet out before them and their backs to the trunk of a tree. On the fire rested their cooking pot, its great lid already quivering as little spurts of water escaped to fall hissing into the flames. A savoury smell arose.

"I can't wait any longer!" exclaimed Loki. Odin smiled as he closed his keen blue eye. Loki jumped up and, running to the fire, took a look at the stew. He seized a pointed stick to lift out one of the shoulders. "Raw!" he said in disgust. "Still perfectly raw!" He banged down the lid.

Odin smiled again. Silence fell. The skylark was weary, but the melodious thrush began her evening song. The grass was golden with buttercups. A kingfisher flashed over the stream. The smell of cooking became very pleas- ant and caused Odin to open his eye. "You might try the stew now," he said to Loki. "I should think we have given

it enough time."

"I do all the work," grumbled Loki, but he got up and went to the fire. "Raw!" he said again in a fury.

This time Odin was interested and sat up straight. "Surely not," he remarked.

"Look at it!" cried Loki brandishing a piece on his stick. "Still as red as it was when we put it in. It's not right!"

"It certainly is strange," replied Odin. "Well, put it back and pile up the fire."

"I am faint with hunger," complained Loki, "and everything falls on me." He piled on some more wood, still grumbling, before he came back and flung himself down on the grass.

A long time passed. The sun was behind the hills by now, and Odin drew his blue cloak about him. The three gods dozed no more, but sat with their hungry eyes fixed on the iron pot. "If it is not done by now, it never will be," said Odin at last. He got up himself, but he fared no better than Loki. The meat smelt appetizing, and the water was boiling and bubbling around it. Nevertheless when Odin lifted a piece from the pot, he found it raw and cold. "There is some magic spell at work here," he declared.

"I can cook your meat," cried a hoarse voice from above them. The three gods looked up. High in the oak tree sat an eagle so huge that the great branch bent beneath his weight like a tiny twig. "Give me a portion of your supper," he said. "Let me take my choice before you begin, and the meal shall be done in an instant."

"Willingly," answered Odin, uncovering the pot once more.

The creature leapt into the air with a whirring of his wings and came sailing down to the fire, claws and beak outstretched. Quickly he snatched up half of the ox and was back in the tree with his dripping burden before the gods could utter a sound. He lay his prey in a fork of the tree and swooped again to seize the other half, leaving the gods nothing but water.

Loki was beside himself with passion. "You thief!" he screamed, and snatching up one of the branches he had laid by to replenish the fire, he struck the eagle as it turned to make for the oak. The branch hit the bird full on the back and stuck there as if glued, while Loki's hands adhered to the other end. The creature gave a sharp screech of laughter and flew off, dragging Loki after him. He skimmed over the ground so that the unfortunate god was pulled over stones and through briars, yelling that his arms were being torn from their sockets.

In a second or two his shrieks were already faint, and in another moment the pair were over the hills and out of earshot. "Let him go," said Odin, "and we will slaughter another ox. I can do nothing for Loki, who is in the power of a giant. He is cunning enough to get free from a dozen enchantments and will certainly join us again before we come to our journey's end."

Sure enough, on the next day Loki met them. He was covered with scratches, and the knees of his leggings were in holes, but he was well enough, though sulky.

"How did you get away?" asked his companions.

"He dropped me after a while," said Loki sullenly. "I suppose he had enough of it. My arms were almost pulled off."

"It is strange that he let you go without a ransom," said Odin.

"Well he did," lied Loki, "although he might have dragged me forever for all the help I got from you." He

strode on ahead, looking around furiously from time to time to see that the two gods were not laughing together behind his back.

The next day Idun, the goddess of youth, was sitting in her attic chamber in Asgard, looking out from her window at the flowering cherry trees. It was always spring in Idun's garden, where the scent of white mayflower lay heavy on the air. A cuckoo called in the distance, and on the window ledge perched a robin close by the goddess's hand. She looked round to see Loki entering, and her fair blue eyes lit up with a smile. Even Loki, the faithless one, was welcome to Idun, who loved and trusted all.

"You have been on a long journey, Loki," she said gaily, "and I think you have come back for an apple from me." With that she picked up a little gold casket from the bench by her side. She put her hand in and took out an apple for him, all rosy and golden. From it came a savour so sweet that with a flutter of wings the birds in the orchard came flocking to her window. Blackbirds, starlings and doves jostled one another for space on the ledges, yet dared not come in, for fair Idun raised her arm and gently barred their path.

As Loki bit into the apple, his bruises felt sore no longer. The fruits of Idun, which were the apples of youth, sent new strength through his limbs. A wild desire seized him to go out in the sunlight, to wrestle, to swim, or even to start another of these toilsome journeys which Odin loved to make through the world.

Idun turned to the casket and shut it. As she did so, there was a faint, musical sound. "Can you hear it?" she asked. "There is already another apple within."

"Idun," said Loki earnestly, "these are wonderful fruits, but out in the forest is a tree with apples of silver and gold. Music plays through its branches, which bear blossoms as sweet as the wild rose together with the marvellous fruit. You know we eat your apples daily to keep us young, but they say that one of these others will bring immortal youth which needs no renewal."

"It is not true," cried Idun, blushing indignantly. "There are no apples better than mine."

"Come out into the woods and look, then," begged Loki. "Bring your casket with you that we may compare the fruits."

"We must go in secret," said she. "I cannot believe you, and I would not have it said that I doubted my apples at all."

Loki and Idun stole out of Asgard into the wild, dark woods. "Come this way, Idun," said Loki, smiling at her as he put his hand on her arm.

"The sun is sinking," said Idun. "Is the tree very far

away?"

"Not so far, and the moon is rising. Besides, the golden fruit will light our path." He guided her up a steep hill. "From the top where it is rocky and bare," said he, "you can look down into the next valley and see the tree gleam. From there our road will be easy." He hurried her up the slope.

The sun had quite disappeared when Idun stood on the rock gazing out over the valley, which was half hidden in the gathering dark. "Why, there is no light to be seen!" said she in a disappointed tone. Loki made no answer, but stood looking up at the faint stars.

"Thjasse! Great Thjasse!" cried he.

"Loki," said she anxiously, pulling at his arm. "Loki, there is no light in the valley, and a cloud is covering the moon!"

"Thjasse! Great Thjasse!" cried Loki again. "Here is Idun, the ransom I promised when you released me from the stick. Take her and let me go home."

There was no cloud over the moon, only the wings of an enormous eagle. Idun could see his red eyes and the great claws outstretched. She screamed and covered her face as the monster clutched her. Loki heard cry after cry as the two vanished into the dark.

Next morning the gods who came to the garden of Idun found it deserted, but at first they were in no way alarmed. "She is visiting Gerd or Freyja," they said to one another. "Tomorrow she will surely be here."

The next day Idun was still absent, and in seven days she had still not returned. The blossoms on her trees had turned brown, the birds had all fled and a chill had crept into the air. Without the magic apples of youth, Odin's hair became straggly and thin. Thor's bushy beard was streaked with grey. Fair Freyja stayed indoors, or veiled her face if she needed to walk abroad.

At last the gods met in council. All denied any knowledge of Idun, Loki among the rest. "Well, then," said Odin, "where did each one of you see her last?"

Nearly all the gods had seen her last in her chamber or her garden. One, however, replied, "Idun stole out of Asgard with Loki as though they wished to escape unseen."

All turned on Loki. Thor clutched him tightly by the shoulder until he cried out.

"Let me go," he cried. "I will confess that I gave her to Thjasse, the giant. It was he who, disguised as an eagle, dragged me on the end of a stick. Odin left me to ransom my life as best I could, so I promised him Idun. What else could I do?"

"Let me crush him," shouted Thor.

"By no means," answered Allfather Odin. "Release him. I think he has spoken well. Loki freed himself from the giant, but the price he paid was too high. It remains for him to rescue sweet Idun or else perish at the hands of Thor."

"Freyja," cried Loki, "lend me your garment of feathers. I will fly as a falcon to Giantland and return with fair Idun or die."

Loki flew as a falcon from Asgard, soared over the hills and the valleys, and skimmed over the bottomless sea. At last the grey cliffs of Giantland towered above him, shrouded in mist. He turned and flew to his left hand, seeking some inlet, for the cliffs went up into the clouds where he had no strength to soar. At last he found a place where a great grey river tumbled into the ocean through a gap in the dripping rocks. It seemed a forbidding inlet, but it was welcome to him, for his wings were icy and numb.

He entered the gorge of the river and saw where the hall of the giant, Thjasse, towered on the hillside, a fortress of ice and rock.

The little falcon flew by the base of Thjasse's wall and alighted in a small crevice at its foot where a great bird had once built a nest. He huddled deep in the straw, while the wet mist swirled outside, and the damp icicles dripped slowly from the crags. It was dry in the little hollow, so that presently he found himself rested and warm. "Now for it!" he thought as he crawled out of his hole, launched himself into the air and began the steep climb towards the upper windows where he hoped to find Idun's bower.

The falcon went spiralling upwards past the sheer face of the rocky wall which towered into the sky. Long before he came to the windows, his heart was beating fast, and his wings were failing. Here, however, the stones were smooth, and he could find no perch. Therefore, though he

circled ever more slowly, he had to fly on.

At last it seemed to him that he could go no higher. Every time his circling brought him close to the rock, the same worn stones met his gaze. He glanced despairingly downwards. Nothing was to be seen there but mist. "I dare not fall," he said to himself as with a mighty effort he forced himself higher. This time as he approached the wall, he saw a break in the rock. It was the window of Idun's chamber above the end of the giant's great hall. Hope gave him renewed strength, and with a fierce beating of wings he circled once more, reached the ledge and dropped half dead upon it, close beside Idun's hand.

Idun was sitting huddled up in the corner of a vast chair, her feet a long way up from the stone floor of the chamber, looking out into the mist. Tears ran down her cheeks as she gazed out towards Asgard, thinking of the beautiful earth, of her garden and of the gods who loved her as though she were a daughter to them all. She stretched out her hands to the bird with a cry of delight, dried it softly with her robe, set it on her shoulder and warmed it against her cheek.

"Idun," said Loki at last in gentle tones, "I will take you to Asgard. Do not be afraid to trust me, for I come at the peril of my life."

Idun started at Loki's voice, but she answered eagerly, "I will do anything you wish if you will only carry me away."

"Where is the giant?"

"Gone forth to fish. If the catch is good, he will not return till dark."

"Trust me, then," said Loki from the window ledge. He touched her with the tip of his wing, and in an instant she and her casket shrank to the size of a thumbnail. Loki laid her gently in a walnut shell, and gathering the nut in his claws, leapt into the air.

They were over the grey sea when they came out of the mist and saw the earth as a strip of green on the distant shore. Every moment the hills became clearer until soon they were over the land. Loki cast a long look behind him and saw a black speck far off on the edge of the sky. "It is the eagle!" he said to himself as he flew on like an arrow.

Over the mountains he looked back again. The bird was much nearer by now. He could see its great wings cleaving the air, and terror gave him strength to speed like the wind. When the ramparts of Asgard came into view, he did not need to look back, for he could hear the air whistling through the wings of the eagle behind him. With the fury of despair he raced for home.

"It is Loki!" cried the gods as they crowded the ramparts. "It is Loki, and behind him the eagle."

"Set fire to the ramparts," cried Allfather Odin. "Whether Loki is slain or not, the giant shall never escape."

Swiftly the gods heaped shavings along the walls and stood by with torches. The birds were so close by now that they could see the great beak of the eagle touch the feathers on Loki's tail. Loki felt his enemy and knew at the same time that he was almost home. With a furious

spurt he shot over the ramparts and tumbled like a stone into the courtyard on the other side.

Already the gods had set fire to their shavings, and flames leapt instantly up from the wall. The eagle, coming too fast to stop himself, lurched right through the fire, setting his wings ablaze. Suddenly he fell from the air and alighted in the courtyard in his own shape of a monstrous man with his garments smoking about him and his great beard singed with flame. He glared at them all, bellowing furiously, but before he could rise, Thor swung his hammer, Mjolnir, that never missed its mark.

That night the gods drank to the rescue of Idun, and the death of the giant, while Loki sat boasting among them as if the trouble had been none of his fault in the first place.

Olivia E. Coolidge

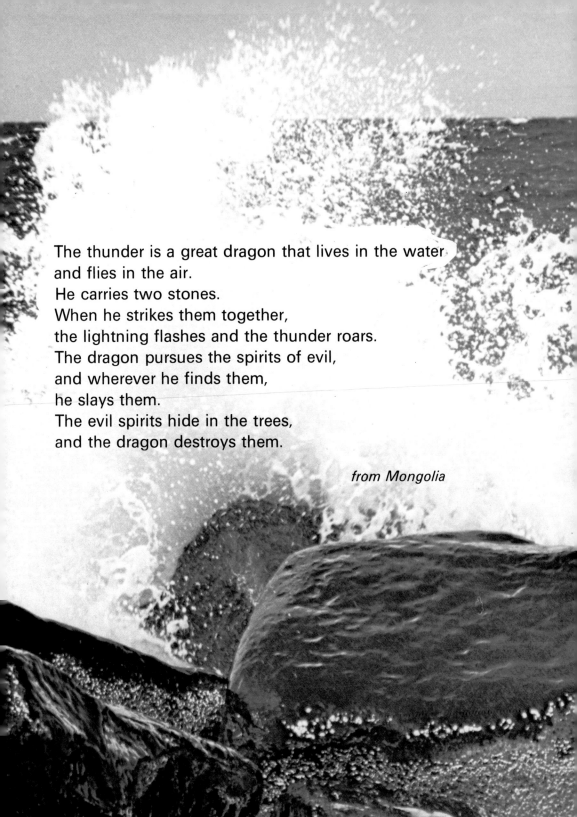

The thunder is a great dragon that lives in the water
and flies in the air.
He carries two stones.
When he strikes them together,
the lightning flashes and the thunder roars.
The dragon pursues the spirits of evil,
and wherever he finds them,
he slays them.
The evil spirits hide in the trees,
and the dragon destroys them.

from Mongolia

The Story of the Creation

In the beginning, when God created the universe, the earth was formless and desolate. The raging ocean that covered everything was engulfed in total darkness, and the power of God was moving over the water. Then God commanded, "Let there be light"—and light appeared. God was pleased with what he saw. Then he separated the light from the darkness, and he named the light "Day" and the darkness "Night". Evening passed and morning came—that was the first day.

Then God commanded, "Let there be a dome to divide the water and to keep it in two separate places"—and it was done. So God made a dome, and it separated the water under it from the water above it. He named the dome "Sky". Evening passed and morning came—that was the second day.

Then God commanded, "Let the water below the sky come together in one place, so that the land will appear"—and it was done. He named the land "Earth", and the water which had come together he named "Sea". And God was pleased with what he saw. Then he commanded, "Let the earth produce all kinds of plants, those that bear grain and those that bear fruit"—and it was done. So the earth produced all kinds of plants, and God was pleased with what he saw. Evening passed and morning came—that was the third day.

Then God commanded, "Let lights appear in the sky to separate day from night and to show the time when days, years and religious festivals begin; they will shine in the sky to give light to the earth"—and it was done. So God made the two larger lights, the sun to rule over the day and the moon to rule over the night; he also made the stars. He placed the lights in the sky to shine on the earth, to rule over the day and the night, and to separate light from darkness. And God was pleased with what he saw. Evening passed and morning came—that was the fourth day.

Then God commanded, "Let the water be filled with many kinds of living beings, and let the air be filled with birds." So God created the great sea-monsters, all kinds of creatures that live in the water, and all kinds of birds. And God was pleased with what he saw. He blessed them all and told the creatures that live in the water to reproduce, and to fill the sea, and he told the birds to increase in number. Evening passed and morning came—that was the fifth day.

Then God commanded, "Let the earth produce all kinds of animal life: domestic and wild, large and small"—and it was done. So God made them all, and he was pleased with what he saw.

Then God said, "And now we will make human beings; they will be like us and resemble us. They will have power over the fish, the birds and all animals, domestic and wild, large and small. So God created human beings, making them to be like himself. He created them male and female, blessed them and said, "Have many children, so that your descendants will live all over the earth and bring it under their control. I am putting you in charge of the fish, the birds and all the wild animals. I have provided all kinds of grain and all kinds of fruit for you to eat; but for all the wild animals and for all the birds I have provided grass and leafy plants for food"—and it was done. God looked at everything he had made, and he was very pleased. Evening passed and morning came—that was the sixth day.

And so the whole universe was completed. By the seventh day God finished what he had been doing and stopped working. He blessed the seventh day and set it apart as a special day, because by that day he had completed his creation and stopped working. And that is how the universe was created.

Good News Bible—Genesis 1, 2:1–4

The Revolt Against God

At the beginning of Things, when there was nothing, neither man, nor animals, nor plants, nor heaven, nor earth, nothing, nothing, God *was* and he was called Nzame. The three who are Nzame, we call Nzame, Mebere and Nkwa. At the beginning Nzame made the heaven and the earth and he reserved the heaven for himself. Then he blew onto the earth and earth and water were created, each on its side.

Nzame made everything: heaven, earth, sun, moon, stars, animals, plants; everything. When he had finished everything that we see today, he called Mebere and Nkwa and showed them his work.

"This is my work. Is it good?"

They replied, "Yes, you have done well."

"Does anything remain to be done?"

Mebere and Nkwa answered him, "We see many animals, but we do not see their chief; we see many plants, but we do not see their master."

As masters for all these things, they appointed the elephant, because he had wisdom; the leopard, because he had power and cunning; and the monkey, because he had malice and suppleness.

But Nzame wanted to do even better; and between them he, Mebere and Nkwa created a being almost like themselves. One gave him force, the second authority and the third beauty. Then the three of them said, "Take the earth. You are henceforth the master of all that exists. Like us you have life, all things belong to you, you are the master."

Nzame, Mebere and Nkwa returned to the heights to their dwelling place, and the new creature remained below alone, and everything obeyed him. But among all the animals the elephant remained the first, the leopard the second and the monkey the third, because it was they whom Mebere and Nkwa had first chosen.

Nzame, Mebere and Nkwa called the first man Fam—which means power.

Proud of his authority, his power and his beauty, because he surpassed in these three qualities the elephant, the leopard and the monkey, and proud of being able to defeat all the animals, this first man grew wicked; he became arrogant, and did not want to worship Nzame again; and he scorned him.

"Yeye, o, layeye,
God on high, man on the earth,
Yeye, o, layeye,
God is God,
Man is man,
Everyone in his house, everyone for himself!"

God heard the song. "Who sings?" he asked.
"Look for him," cried Fam.
"Who sings?"
"Yeye, o, layeye!"
"Who sings?"
"Eh! it is me!" cried Fam.
Furious, God called Nzalan, the thunder. "Nzalan, come!"
Nzalan came running with great noise: boom, boom, boom!
The fire of heaven fell on the forest. The plantations burnt
like vast torches. Foo, foo, foo!—everything in flames. The
earth was then, as today, covered with forests. The trees
burnt; the plants, the bananas, the cassava, even the pistachio
nuts: everything dried up. Animals, birds, fishes, all were
destroyed, everything was dead. But when God had created
the first man, he had told him, "You will never die." And
what God gives he does not take away. The first man was burnt,
but none knows what became of him. He is alive, yes, but
where?

But God looked at the earth, all black, without anything, and idle; he felt ashamed and wanted to do better. Nzame, Mebere and Nkwa took counsel and they did as follows: over the black earth covered with coal they put a new layer of earth; a tree grew, grew bigger and bigger and when one of its seeds fell down a new tree was born, when a leaf severed itself it grew and grew and began to walk. It was an animal, an elephant, a leopard, an antelope, a tortoise—all of them. When a leaf fell into the water it swam, it was a fish, a sardine, a crab, an oyster—all of them. The earth became again what it had been, and what it still is today. The proof that this is the truth is this: when one digs up the earth in certain places, one finds a hard black stone which breaks; throw it on the fire and it burns.

But Nzame, Mebere and Nkwa took counsel again; they needed a chief to command all the animals. "We shall make a man like Fam," said Nzame, "with the same legs and arms, but we shall turn his head and he shall see death."

This was the second man and the father of all. Nzame called him Sekume, but did not want to leave him alone, and said, "Make yourself a woman from a tree."

Sekume made himself a woman and she walked and he called her Mbongwe.

When Nzame made Sekume and Mbongwe he made them

in two parts, an outer part called Gnoul, the body, and the other which lives in the body, called Nsissim.

Nsissim is that which produces the shadow, Nsissim is the shadow—it is the same thing. It is Nsissim who makes Gnoul live. Nsissim goes away when man dies, but Nsissim does not die. Do you know where he lives? He lives in the eye. The little shining point you see in the middle, that is Nsissim.

> Stars above
> Fire below
> Coal in the hearth
> The soul in the eye
> Cloud smoke and death.

Sekume and Mbongwe lived happily on earth and had many children. But Fam, the first man, was imprisoned by God underneath the earth. With a large stone he blocked the entrance. But the malicious Fam tunnelled through the earth for a long time, and one day, at last, he was outside! Who had taken his place? The new man. Fam was furious with him. Now he hides in the forest to kill them, under the water to capsize their boats.

> Remain silent,
> Fam is listening,
> To bring misfortune;
> Remain silent

from Gabon

The Light and the Souls

Before the beginning of time there was God. He was never born nor will he ever die. If he wishes a thing, he merely says to it, "Be!" and it exists.

So God said, "There be light!" And there was light. God took a fistful of this light and it shone in his hand. Then he said, "I am pleased with you, my light, I will make out of you my prophet, I will mould you into the soul of Mohammed."

When he had created the soul of the prophet Mohammed (may God pray for him and give him peace), he loved it so much that he decided to create mankind so that he might send Mohammed to it as his messenger to bring his word to earth. His word would teach the peoples of the earth the distinction between good and evil, and in the end God would judge all the souls and reward those who had chosen to follow the good messenger, and reject the others.

With his infinite knowledge God foresaw all the events that

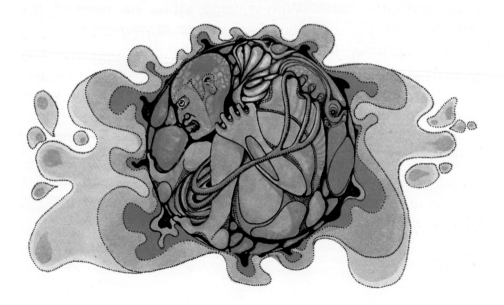

would happen in the centuries to follow until the last day. With his unlimited power God began to create all the things he would need for some purpose which he alone knew.

First he created the throne and the carpet for himself to sit on at the Last Judgment. The throne has four legs supported by four strong beasts. The carpet that covers it has all the lovely colours of the rainbow and stretches out along the skies as far as the borders of space. Under the throne there is the most delightful place in the universe: the souls who are allowed to dwell in the shadow of the carpet will rejoice forever. The brilliant light of the divine presence is softly filtered by the many-coloured veils of which the carpet is composed.

The third thing God created was the well-preserved tablet. It is a board so large that it can contain a complete and detailed description of all the events that ever take place anywhere in past and future. The tablet has a soul of her own and is one of God's most faithful servants. She carries all his wisdom and all his commandments for ever and ever. She is called the mother of books, because all the sacred books of mankind in which God has revealed some of his truth contain only fragments of her contents. The secrets of the universe, in so far as they were ever represented by symbols, are inscribed on her surface, in characters which only he can read.

With the tablet he created the pen to write his commandments. The pen is as long as the distance between heaven and earth. It has a thinking head and a personality, and as soon as it had come into existence, God ordered it, "Write!"

The pen asked, "What shall I write, my Lord?"

God said, "Destiny."

Since that moment the pen has been busy writing on the tablet all the deeds of men.

Of course, if it pleases God to change his mind, he does so. If he projects a different future than was foreseen in previous plans, the writing will disappear from the tablet and the pen will record new facts.

The fifth thing God created was the trumpet, and with it the archangel Serafili (Asrafel). The angel holds the trumpet to his mouth, waiting patiently in the same position, century after century, until it pleases God to terminate history. Then he will give the signal, and Serafili will blow his first blast. The trumpet has such a powerful voice that at its first sound the mountains

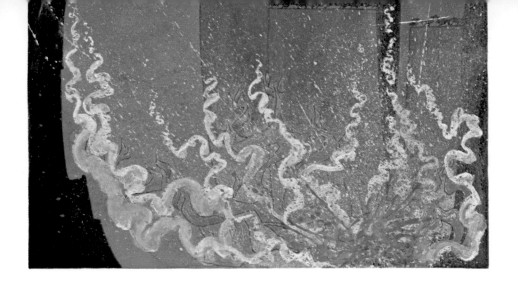

will collapse, the stars will come plummeting down and doomsday will begin.

The sixth thing which God created was the garden of delights which was destined for the good souls. There they would stay for ever and ever, forgetting the sufferings of their lives on earth. In it there are streams of limpid water, rivers of milk and honey, fragrant flowers and trees whose branches bend down heavy with fruits. The fruits are soft and sweet and juicy and as soon as one falls off, a new one grows on the same branch in no time. Who would not give everything he possessed to be there? Who would not endure a short span of life on earth to dwell in that garden for all eternity?

The seventh thing which God created, foreseeing in his wisdom that many souls would not follow the good messenger, was the fire. Crackling, it sprang up from the deepest bottom of shadows, in the remotest pit of space. Evil smell and smoke is its essence, roaring thunder its voice.

"My Lord," cried the fire, "where are the souls of sinners, I want to see them suffer!" Who would not pray night and day that his soul may avoid this eternal torture?

God went on and on creating, taking things out of not-being, for God requires no rest; neither sleep nor slumber seize him.

God now created the angels, a myriad of voices who proclaim his praise. Out of pure light he created them; their minds are as lucid as the light itself, their hearts are as pure as morning air. The thought of sin never occurs to them, they never hatch evil plans in their bosoms. They are as honest as the light that is their element and always shines through their bodies. This is why they are devoted servants of their Lord, and the idea of disobedience cannot arise in their hearts. Their wings are shining white and soft; they tremble with the fear of God.

The first of the archangels is Jiburili (Gabriel) whose task it is to carry God's word to his prophets. Therefore Jiburili is also called the trustworthy spirit.

Tradition says that Mohammed, during his life on earth, asked Jiburili, "Show me your true shape."

Jiburili warned him that this would be dangerous, but Mohammed insisted. Then Jiburili showed himself, and lo, he filled the whole horizon, and his many wings rustled through the skies from east to west. The prophet fainted with fear, and fell. Jiburili lifted him up and said, "Do not fear, I am your

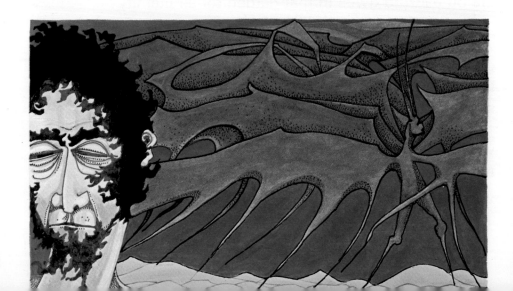

brother Jiburili."

When God had doomed the cities of Lot, he sent Jiburili to destroy them. To this end, Jiburili unfolded two special black wings that spell perdition whenever they appear. With these wings he tore the two cities out of the earth like poisonous toadstools, raised them so high that the inhabitants of heaven could hear their cocks crowing, and then flung them down into the fire.

Mikaili (Michael) is the second archangel. He is in charge of the sustenance of all the creatures of the earth. Thousands of angels serve under his command and are busy day and night. They provide all living beings with all the things they need, according to God's degree. Some will receive plenty, others may starve, and he alone knows the reason. No mortal being need fear that he will not receive his due. What God has destined for him will come to him: air to breathe, water to drink, food to eat, partners to procreate with. We do not have to look for these things; they will be brought to us. We are all like beggars sitting at the Lord's door, and praying that he may throw us a few coins daily.

Serafili, the angel of the trumpet, has already been mentioned. His task is simply to wait for the signal of the end.

Zeraili (Azrael) is the angel of death, the taker of souls, who brings each creature the last message. He obeys God alone, he commands kings and caliphs, jinns and giants, and they all follow him humbly into the unknown.

Maliki is the guardian of the fire in which the sinful souls, the hypocrites and heathens, are punished. His face is terrible to see; he is created out of the glowing clouds of God's wrath.

Ridhuani is the custodian of paradise. He opens its seven gates whenever God thus orders him, so that a thousand pleasant smells are spread out over the earth.

Many other angels live in heaven, more than we can know. There is an angel with a thousand heads: each head has a thousand mouths and every mouth proclaims God's glory in a different language.

There is an angel whose left half is fire, and his right half snow; the snow does not extinguish the fire, nor the fire melt the snow, because God wills it so. At his order two opposing elements can exist side by side; and he can make enemies meet.

There is also a cock in heaven: its feet are on the lowest level of paradise but its head is above the seventh level. Its function is to crow at the precise moment God has destined for the prayer of dawn. Every morning before sunrise it crows jubilantly, flapping its wings, and all the angels of heaven immediately assemble for the morning prayer. Its joyful sound can be heard on earth by all the cocks, on the farms as well as in the bush, and they all repeat it, encouraging each other. This is a sign for men to rise from their couches and prepare themselves for the first prayer of the day.

from East Africa

Heaven and Earth

When God's moment had come, he began creating the world
of matter. He rolled out the day-sky and the night-sky like an
immense tent, or like carpets full of mysterious signs and
symbols. In the night-sky he placed the fixed stars like lamps
with motionless flames. Others move along the sky, each following a path which only he knows. The moon too travels
along the night-sky, changing its shape as he wishes. In the
radiant blue day-sky, he placed the glowing sun and ordered
her to rise in the east, travel along the sky and set in the west.
He created clouds, and painted them in different colours, to sail
like ships along the day-sky; toward evening he makes them
glow red. Some are dark and heavy with rain which he will
shower over the lands he wishes to bear fruit.

He constructed the universe in seven heavens, the seventh
being the lowest level of paradise. Each heaven has its own
planet, the lowest being the moon. The second heaven is ruled
by Mercury, the third by Venus, the fourth by Mars, the fifth
by Jupiter, the sixth by Saturn and the seventh by the Sun.
The guardians of these heavens are the souls of eight prophets

of God. They are Adam in the first heaven, Isa (Jesus) and his cousin Yahya (John the Baptist), together in the second, Yusufu (Joseph) in the third, Idirisi (Enoch) in the fourth, Haruni (Aaron) in the fifth and Musa (Moses) in the sixth. Abraham is the guardian of the seventh heaven; his station is near the wall of the celestial mosque where 70,000 angels come to pray every day—and they are never the same ones.

Opposite the high heavens, there are the deep hells, seven layers of them, each one more terrible than the one above it, each one destined for a particular type of sinner. In the deepest hell, farthest away from their maker, will dwell the unbelievers, who will be tortured there eternally.

Then God spread out the earth, like a carpet for men to sit on during their meal. For the earth is full of food for all the creatures of the Lord. And he caused some parts to be barren sands, but wherever he wished, he made grass sprout for the hoofed animals, and trees for the monkeys, and fruit-bearing vegetation with colourful products, a pleasure for the tongue.

He divided the land from the sea, creating the immeasurable ocean on one side, and the high walls of the continents on the other. He heaped up the rocks to be menacing mountains, then told the streams to rush down them in crystal torrents.

He sowed the islands, to be colourful bouquets growing out of the ocean and a pleasure for the sailing skippers. He commanded quiet pools to reflect the blue skies and the mighty

rivers to spread out over the marshes.

He gave a voice to the wind, so that it can whisper as well as roar while it travels over the countries. It pushes the clouds in all directions and it carries the birds on its powerful back. It blows the ships to their destination and it whips up the waves into a frenzy.

Then he told the earth to teem with insects, and lo, a hundred thousand kinds crawled through the sand and flew up into the air on diaphanous wings. The butterflies flutter and the beetles creep; they all have the symbols of their maker written on their backs. Then he released swarms of birds who flew joyfully into the air. Some sat down on branches to praise their maker with songs in unknown languages. Others built their nests, and he alone was their teacher.

Then he told the ocean to be full of fishes of different forms, and so it happened. Only he knows how many there are — and they all have different colours. Then he told the lizards to exist and they obeyed, basking in his sunshine, and the croaking frogs who praise the Lord in their own language. Only he knows how many there are and how many eggs they must lay.

Then the merciful maker called to the heavy animals to come into existence and they did, praising him by lowing and bleating. He created the flesh-eating beasts with claws, and the howling ones which eat carrion. He designed the quiet giraffe and the irascible buffalo, herds of antelope and striped donkeys, the river-dwelling hippopotamus and the gigantic elephant.

Only he knows how many species there are; he knows the

colour of every feather, the sharpness of every tooth. He created the herds of docile cows, their bulging udders full of milk, and the strong-legged camels who travel without thirst. He decided the life-span of the butterfly, and he lit the glowing light of the fire-fly. He decided the law of his creation: that the small fishes will be eaten by the big ones, and they in their turn swallowed by yet bigger fishes. The vultures will descend from the sky to pick the bones of those that die. He makes green leaves for the goats, he makes the dove unaware of the swift swoop of the hawk. He gives the dead bodies to the worms and maggots, then he gives the worms to the chickens and the unsuspecting chicken to the bateleur eagle, who flies up with it into the pillarless sky.

He caused all his creatures to grow and multiply. Fresh green grass stalks sprout after every bush fire; smooth reddish mangoes bulge every year between the dark green leaves of the mother tree.

In every rainy season the white ants swarm out, rustling in their myriads like the first heavy showers. The black ants march along their own roads, hatching their young in their mounds. Which animal is there that does not have children? The baboon babies cling to their mothers' breasts, the long-legged giraffe suckles his mother. What is there that he has forgotten? Are all these miracles not signs to you of his infinite wisdom, of his immense power?

from East Africa

Glossary

accordingly   therefore

arrogantly   haughtily; proudly

bateleur eagle   large African eagle

caliph   Muslim Chief; civil and religious ruler

carrion   dead rotten flesh

cassava   tropical plant with tuberous roots from which flour is made

celestial   heavenly

consume   to eat up; to use; to destroy

cormorant   large, diving sea bird with an excessive appetite

diaphanous   light and delicate, almost transparent

distinction   *1* difference *2* outstanding merit

ebb   outward movement of tide

enchantment   magic charm or spell

engulf   to swallow up wholly

Gorgon (*Greek myth.*)   one of three snake-haired sisters

heathen   person who does not believe in any of the major world religions

henchman   trusty follower

hoary   white or grey with age

hospitality   kindly welcome; friendly treatment

hypocrite   person who pretends to be better than he is, or to be what he is not

inscribe   to write in or on

intricate   complicated; difficult to follow or understand

irascible   easily angered

jinn   mythical spirit

limpid   clear or transparent

linden   lime tree

malice   spite; ill will

melancholy   low spirits; sadness

myriad   very great number; numberless

oracle   *1* (*in ancient times*) supposed answer from a god in reply to a difficult question *2* person of great wisdom

perdition   eternal death or damnation

pistachio   tree yielding nut with greenish edible kernel

prevail   *1* to gain victory (over or against) *2* to persuade *3* to be usual

procreate to produce offspring

prowess courage; bravery; great skill or ability

rampart bank of earth, sometimes with a wall on the top built as a defence

realm *1* kingdom *2* part or section of human knowledge, action, experience, etc.

renounce to give up or reject publicly

replenish to fill up again

savoury pleasant to smell or taste

scorn to look down on; to despise; to refuse or reject with contempt

sickle tool with curved blade and short handle used to cut grain, grass, etc.

stripling a youth

suckling unweaned child or animal

suppleness flexibility; pliability

surpass to be better than

sustenance food or nourishment

temple *1* building in which people pray and worship *2* flat part of either side of head between forehead and ear

Titan (*Greek myth.*) member of a race of giants

troth loyalty or fidelity

victor person who wins a battle, contest, etc.

wrath violent anger